The Mental Breakdown

Sammy,
You're such a
jewel. Always shine
your light! xoxo

Copyright & Permissions

Permissions

The Mental Breakdown

by Alana R. Higginbotham

DEDICATION

This book and every ounce of work it took to birth it out is dedicated to my parents, John and Paulette Renè and to my husband and children; Damon, Drew and Dean Higginbotham.

Through their hard work, persistence and love my parents gave me all the tools necessary to be great and affective in this world. There unwavering commitment to grow me into a respectful, conscious and compassionate human gave legs to my vision of helping others be greater versions of themselves. My dad gave me a work ethic and fearlessness that is unmatched. My mom gave me a fun, bright and forgiving perspective on life that made me both the life of the party and a shoulder to cry on.

I owe my life and my living to the tremendous sacrifices they made and no book dedication could ever come close to matching that in appreciation. This work is as much theirs as it is mine.

They are my cornerstones.

To my husband and children I owe gratitude for their grace. It takes grace to give your wife and mom the space to create a work to save others. They gave me room to work and love to manifest it all.

My husband has been my best cheerleader and biggest coach. His love and compassion got me through my darkest times. He is God's love in human form.

My oldest son Drew has been that extra push I needed at times as well as that extra 'atta girl' when I didn't know I needed it. He makes me a better person so he can be a better person.

My youngest son Dean gives the best hugs and kisses when I need them most. He helps me stay focused because I know he needs to see his mom go out and do great things to give him the courage to be fearless.

This is our book.

TABLE OF CONTENTS

CHAPTER 1
HOW YOUR THOUGHTS BECOME THINGS

CHAPTER 2
THE ROOT OF THOSE THOUGHTS

CHAPTER 3
THE AFTERMATH OF THOSE THOUGHTS

CHAPTER 4
THE REMEDY

CHAPTER 5
THE PRESCRIPTION

INTRODUCTION

I spent a lot of years with a pretty-looking life while I fought through the hell of my own thoughts. I lived many days feeling worthless while looking flawless. Wait … let's be honest, I was convinced I was worthless.

I ate my way through pain and uncertainty, yet I always showed up with a smile for those who needed me. Meanwhile, every evening, I retreated to a place with no second chances, no grace, no peace, and no understanding.

I was living what truly was a fairytale: a very handsome husband who loved me, two beautiful and healthy children who adored me and a host of friends, family and acquaintances who admired my wit, applauded my confidence and sought my advice. I was so good at it.

Honestly, it was really real. I really did have all of those great and wonderful things. I really did have a great insight about life that I applied to help a lot of people. I just wasn't able to use it for myself.

I enjoyed being around people. I loved talking with women about their lives, offering a positive, yet stern and real perspective for them to consider. It was like stepping out of hell for just a moment while I gave my positive vibes to those around me and kept none for myself. As soon as the event was over, when I returned, either physically or mentally, to my **perceived reality**, my **head trash** took over again.

perceived reality, *noun*

:the world around you as YOU see it (often differs from actual reality; what is really or actually in the world around you).

head trash, *noun*

:the negative thoughts that take up space in your mind like garbage in a landfill, leaving no room for positive thinking.

> *"You're fat", "You're' not a good mom",*
> *"Your husband is with you because he*
> *feels sorry for you."*

These thoughts become your reality when you allow them to manifest in that direction. You move around honestly believing that people, many of whom you don't even know, are looking at you thinking the same crazy thoughts about you that you think about yourself. You begin to attract those types of people to your experience. You believe you are selfish or at least that's what you tell yourself, so you begin to attract selfish people to you. You know the ones I'm referring to. The ones you bend over backwards for. The ones you lose several hours of sleep over because you were up working on a project for them. They are the very people who turn around and call you selfish because maybe you chose to visit your mom in the hospital instead of showing up to their birthday brunch.

My goal is to introduce you to the power that you've had all along to change your position in life. Further, my goal is to not just change your position, but change the way you think about your position and give you a clear picture on how to use this power to MOVE … wherever you want to go.

REALITY CHECK:

*None of this "new life, new level" business is going to happen JUST because you change the way you think. You're going to have to work at the "doing" of it all. It's not going to change the requirements of your goal. You're still going to need to pass the bar to be a lawyer. You'll just have the belief in yourself, the vision of victory and the **mental fortitude** to make it happen.*

mental fortitude, *noun*

:the state of having strong thoughts that overcome challenges

:the ability to focus on and execute solutions in the face of uncertainty or adversity. (Entrepreneur Magazine)

Ex: *To push past adversity and endure, she used her mental fortitude.*

No matter where you are, no matter what you are doing, one thing is certain: the way you manage your thoughts got you there.

This book is going to show you how to use your thoughts to get you somewhere else.

REALITY CHECK:

You don't have to be in a bad place to want to move forward. It may be something as fundamental as wanting to do bigger and better things. Either way, physical motion requires **mental readiness***.*

mental readiness, *noun*

:the quality of and state of being mentally ready

:having a mind and thoughts prepared for proper execution of a goal

Ex: *His mental readiness was surely the key to his promotion.*

Let's get started, shall we?

CHAPTER 1
How Your Thoughts Become Things

Merriam-Webster defines breakdown as:

a. a failure of function

b. failure to progress or have effect

c. the process of decomposing

d. division into categories

All of these are true for the purposes of this lesson.

Have you noticed that what you focus on manifests in your life? Actually, what you focus on is magnified. It was there all along but your focus on it brings it from the background into the foreground.

Here's an example. You recently bought a Lexus. Suddenly, you see them everywhere. There has not been a dramatic increase in your area in Lexus ownership over the past year, it's just that you more clearly see the ones that have always been around you. So, the pool of great guys was always there, right next to the toxic guys, all along. There's no shortage of good jobs or great girls. Your mental focus is what creates the landscape of your life. It's sort of like a magic trick.

Magicians often use sleight-of-hand, distraction and mind manipulation to take the things that are already around you and make you see them differently or not at all. This is similar to how you can train yourself to properly handle your thoughts and thereby create your desired environment.

There are habits you have that you likely don't know are habits. There are behaviors you insist on maintaining that aren't good for you. There is a point where the carousel slows and even stops to let you off, but the comfort of sameness won't allow you to reach for or even notice there is a way out. You're the one with the control.

Your mind is constantly focusing on what you consider to be random thoughts. But they aren't random at all. They levitate from deep in your thought bank and float across your consciousness. What you do with those thoughts create the life in and around you.

STORY TIME:

It works like your Netflix account. Based on the things you've chosen in the past, your account gives you suggestions of what to watch next. The only way to change that is to change your choices. You'll need to start doing something different. You have to choose something different to get a different outcome.

Thinking about what you want, no matter how unattainable it seems, will give you thoughts that you can capture to create a world around you filled with better choices.

If you've ever taken a multiple choice test where the choices made the correct answer obvious, you already understand what it'll be like when you start handling your thoughts better.

You will see the choice that's best for you rising up to meet your reality. The universe will make everything else around you blurry while your perfect choice is in full focus.

Keep in mind, your perfect choice will either come to perfect you or prepare you.

Perfecting you may include a lesson to be learned or a challenge to overcome. Preparing you will be more like dressing you for the occasion of stepping into your new level/environment. Which ever one of those comes forth it is exactly what you need for wherever you are on your journey. Be open, be embracing and don't ever think of any of it as losing. It's all part of the course you're taking to get what you want.

Welcome the challenges. Open up to the discomfort. All of it shapes you, grows you and molds you into the person that can receive and retain all the levels in life you want to achieve.

Everything won't be hard. But it will be challenging to the degree you need it to be. Let it take you to the place you have to be to get what you want.

Knowing how your thoughts work or can work will help you tremendously. You have to practice **mindful thinking**.

mindful thinking, *verb*

    :producing   concentrated   thoughts   through deliberate focus

Ex: *She used her mindful thinking to achieve new results.*

Be conscious. Start your days focusing on what you want to happen in your day, week, month, year and life. Use the night before to map what you want to think about. It's like laying out what you want to wear the night before. Lay out your thoughts the night before. Plan your thoughts the way you plan a year of goals. Train your mind to produce good thoughts that will turn into good opportunities for a great **life landscape.**

life landscape, *noun*

    :the world as it exists around you, whether real or perceived

Ex: *My life landscape changed when I put my new mindset into practice.*

I hear you out there. You're thinking, ***"Alana, I know I have issues. Now, what the hell do I do to fix them?"*** Well, I sure am glad you asked! Keep on reading.

LET'S BREAK IT DOWN:

> ➢ We have a habit of focusing on the things we want to change more than the things we actually want.

➢ We go about our days constantly playing in our head the details that we want to get rid of in every area of our lives.

➢ Example: We may start on the drive to work thinking about the kids' school projects that it seems we'll never finish. Then, we think about the weight we'll gain over the coming holidays (we haven't gained it yet and we're already disgusted about it). Then BOOM, we notice the crack in the windshield that we don't have time to fix. Plus, Bae been trippin' about everything lately and we're over it all.

WHEW, I'm exhausted just typing it. We just spent what could have been a great drive with a great cup of coffee instead chewing on all the bitter things we don't actually want in our lives. By doing so, we're creating more of that which we don't want.

The way you handle your thoughts changes:

- the way you respond
- the decisions you make
- how you show up
- the people, places and things that are drawn to you
- what you require
- what you expect
- your health, wealth and relationships

And so much more…

When you think a thing and hold that thought in your consciousness it's like a seed taking root right before your eyes. It wasn't true before but you've made it true because of what you did with that thought when it popped into your head.

Example:

You're trying to complete a project and the deadline looms. You're trying to wrap it up when your kid throws up on the upstairs sofa. Your husband is looking for his passport for the third time this week and needs your help. Someone spilled pancake mix on the floor and you're searching for the mop because the mini vacuum you normally use lost battery power. You think to yourself,

> ### *"Why does all this stuff always come up when I'm on deadline?"*

The truth is that those things happen when you don't have a looming deadline. Another truth, you've had more than one occasion where your deadline was uninterrupted and you had the chance to focus on your task with no distractions.

Don't make your current view into a story of how life always is, or that's exactly what you'll get. Not because it is reality, but because you turned it into *your* reality by mishandling your thoughts.

To create a different reality, you'll have to be deliberate about harnessing your thoughts and consciously practice doing so.

It's important for you to understand that none of the decisions that you make are incorrect. You have never actually made a mistake. You've made decisions based on the information and the level of understanding you had at the time. Knowing this gives you a sense that you're not navigating unknown territory.

You actually are fully aware of your surroundings, and you have an understanding of what you need in the moment that the decision has to be made. You were created with everything necessary for you to be where you want to be rather than where you find yourself.

The world around you gives you a set of requirements. People in that world tell you what you need to do based on what they need from you. Sometimes that doesn't line up with what's in your soul and your spirit. The reason you feel lazy, unproductive and unfulfilled is because you have allowed other people and situations to tell you where to go and what to do. Allow yourself to decide what makes you happy and fulfilled.

It is important that you believe in your capacity to make good decisions for yourself. Every decision you make is the right decision for that moment, even if it gives you an outcome you do not like. It is the outcome that you need for the growth that is necessary to get to your next level. If you had not made that *"mistake,"* you would not have been able to learn the lesson that it taught you.

You see, thoughts become things and every day, we send them out into the world to create the landscape of our lives. So, the view from where you sit is of your own creation. Now, what's the beauty of that? It's that you can create it to look like whatever you wish. All you need to do is concentrate.

REALITY CHECK:

You're not going to advance your life by making the same mistake over and over again. You have to pay attention to patterns. As soon as you notice *"I've been here before"* make a change in how you handle your thoughts to change your outcome.

STORY TIME:

Alice has *a fear of failing the bar exam. She's a great student and earned top grades in law school. She hired a tutor and joined a study group to prepare for the bar. But, all she can think about is the horror stories she's heard of people taking the bar time and time again and failing. She focuses on this so much that she even has dreams of failing. She comes from a long line of attorneys who passed the bar on the first try, but something in her keeps capturing the thought of failing and instead of switching to what could happen if she passes, she focuses dreadfully on the failure of this important exam. She prepares for it. She studies. She goes through a checklist to make sure that she's able to retain the information that she is studying.*

Alice takes the bar and fails. She's in utter disbelief. She can't comprehend that all of her efforts were worthless. She talks with a close friend who tells Alice she's been mishandling her thoughts. She gives her a plan of action to focus on.

Here's the plan: Alice's friend suggests she focus on what would happen if she did pass the bar. What would it look like? What would she be wearing when she heard the news? She suggested Alice picture herself getting a good night's sleep the night before, eating a good breakfast, getting ready, driving to the test location.

Alice didn't do any extra studying. She focused and focused on passing the bar. For months that was her only task. No tutors, no checklists, just every day visualizing herself passing the bar and celebrating when she got the news.

Guess what happened? Alice passed the bar! Why? Because she changed how she handled her thoughts. The only thing that was holding her back was the way she thought about herself. That doesn't mean that thoughts of failing did not come up. It means that she handled those thoughts better by pushing them aside and refocusing on success.

She didn't have confidence in herself to pass the bar because she focused on dreadful stories, like the one gentleman in Mississippi who took the bar 36 times before he passed. It was the head trash she let in that put her at a disadvantage.

When you come up against a challenge, stay focused on all the positive things that can happen. It's already a given that bad things may happen, challenges will arise, and mistakes can be made. So put those thoughts to the side and focus on all that it can be if and when it goes right.

It will change the way you manage challenges, change the way you make decisions, and eventually change the outcome.

REFLECTIVE EXERCISE

1. On a piece of paper, list the top five things you would like to change in your life right now.

2. On the same piece of paper, list the top five things you believe are holding you back from moving forward on those changes.

3. If those hindrances did not exist, would you move forward on making the changes?

4. Draw a big X across the list of hindrances.

5. Draw a circle around the things you wish to change.

    1. Read through that list three times.

    2. Put the paper away, sit back, close your eyes, and think about what your life would look like if all those things changed.

    3. Do this for 60 seconds

       (think about every detail: what you are wearing, how the sun is shining, what the air smells like)

I'm sure you feel the difference. Nothing in your life has officially changed yet, but your optimism has grown because you got a taste of what the success would feel like if you were able to make those changes.

If you took the time to reflect daily on the outcome you desire and to sit in what that feels, looks, or even tastes like, you would move closer to that reality.

Simple, right? Let's press on and learn a little more to strengthen your resolve and your will to make the changes and get the goal.

Laying Out Your Thoughts

1. Search the internet for pictures of what you want your situation/life to look like.

2. You can screenshot what you find and put it into a note or text to yourself.

3. You can type captions for the pictures as well as quotes, scripture passages or words of encouragement.

4. Treat it like a digital vision board.

5. Pull it up and look through it before you lay your head on the pillow to sleep every night.

6. Leave it up on your phone so its the first thing you see when you unlock your phone. (all of this can also be done on your computer or tablet)

7. Pull it up before you even allow your feet to hit the floor in the morning and before you do any meditation or prayer. This will get your mind focused and you can include these things in your meditation and prayer.

CHAPTER 2

THE ROOT OF THOSE THOUGHTS

Root is defined as:

(noun)

    a. the part of a plant that attaches it to the ground or to a support, typically underground, conveying water and nourishment to the rest of the plant via numerous branches and fibers

    b. the basic cause, source, or origin of something

(verb)

    a. cause (a plant or cutting) to grow roots

    b. establish deeply and firmly

Many of the ways in which we do things as adults stem from experiences in our childhood. As simple as the way we order in restaurants or as complex as how we decide on a mate, we get our **Matrix Of Thought** (don't worry, I'll explain that later) from foundations we learned or unlearned as children.

Our level of trust, our ability to process occurrences, our comfort level with new things and even our outlook on self come from our early years and what we have accepted as truth. Whatever your brain processes, it does at the level you were when the ideal for that topic was introduced. Just think, many of us are walking around using the ideals of a seven-year-old to process the experiences of a forty-year-old. Maybe you watched the hurt your mom experienced when your dad left when you were seven. You created an ideal at that age of what you were going to do to either never experience that hurt or never cause it. This is why you see many adults acting immaturely in adult circumstances. Their decision-making process never matured. You become an adult with a seven-year-old decision-making strategy. There are so many things that a seven-year-old can't grasp or understand because their brain is still developing. Seven-year-olds aren't equipped to successfully decide adult matters. However, it happens all the time in so many situations. The tragedy is that we often don't even realize there is a problem. We don't see that our desire, for example, to have a mate is hinging on changing or growing our mindset. We often don't realize that one area of mental immaturity filters into a completely different area of life.

"You just have to trust the process while you continue to work the plan."

STORY TIME:

A woman, we'll call her Liz, orders a meal while dining in a restaurant.

There with her children, she's insistent on getting a to-go cup for her drinks and plastic utensils for her meals.

You see, Liz doesn't know it, but this behavior is a **coping mechanism** to not only make her feel safe but to make her feel like she's protecting her children. In her mind, it counteracts the inconsistency of her own mother, who did not routinely protect and secure her as a child. She doesn't even realize that this act is mostly futile, considering that the same employees she doesn't trust to give her safe, clean cups and silverware are the same ones in charge of cooking the food she and her children are about to eat.

Liz spent her childhood as the primary caregiver for her younger siblings. Still in elementary school, she developed a routine for mothering her siblings at the end of the school day. She started dinner, washed a load of clothes, and directed her little brothers and sisters to their own tasks. She did all this while listening to the unsafe environment outside her kitchen window.

Liz and her siblings spent most of their time alone while their mom figured out life amidst drug use and a string of abusive relationships. Liz craved safety, and at an age that most kids depend on their parents to provide it, she developed her own safe practices. She was a deep thinker and constantly mulled over scenarios on how to best protect herself from harms both seen and unseen. She made silent pacts with herself about the kind of mother she would be and how she would, at all costs, protect her children far and beyond the lack of protection she experienced as a kid.

Liz focused so much on the task of protection and got such a great feeling of accomplishment from developing a new protective process that she never considered how much trouble and stress all these new routines were adding to her life. She was so keen on being safe and not turning out like her mother that she never realized she was only making life tougher for herself and her children.

Her coping mechanism was doing the opposite of what she created it to do. Instead, of simplifying her life it was adding more chaos and only creating an illusion of safety. Just like the act of demanding paper cups and plastic eating utensils is really not keeping her safe from the germs of the restaurant, her safety routines aren't truly keeping her safe. They are merely making her feel less like her mom and more responsible than her mom. The fulfillment she is getting is coming from the routine of being different than the irresponsible caregivers she grew up with, but she isn't really any safer.

Simplify your life. Give yourself permission to let go and just live and experience life. Sometimes safety nets keep us from experiences that will enrich our lives. For every step you take to distance yourself from your past you collect experiences that keep you mentally stuck there. In reality you are repeating your past in a way that keeps you from recognizing your mistakes.

Be free to actually live your life.

coping mechanism, *noun*

:an adaptation to environmental stress that is based on conscious or unconscious choice and that enhances control over behavior or gives psychological comfort (dictionary.com).

REALITY CHECK:

You are not going to visualize yourself skinny and then wake up skinny. But, the pathway to a slimmer body is to visualize your acceptance of your current body image. What if being fat isn't bad? What if being fat is a positive thing? What if your body actually looks nice when you carry it the right way? Get an understanding of your current state first, and then you can plan and process through to the next level. The one you desire.

It's important to note that while it is easier to pick out the discrepancies in others, it's more effective when we analyze ourselves. This is because self is the only factor we have control over. It can be real tough realizing that you have responsibility in your own demise BUT...the great news is that also means it's in your power to change it and make it like you want it.

Let's look into our ambitions and desires. It's very common to feel or recognize a desire in ourselves then talk ourselves out of why we should have or go for it. It's mainly because our desires come from a deep place of unconsciousness and most often, show up way before the provisions to execute those desires do. Basically, it seems impossible or at least highly unlikely.

Those desires actually come from a deep pocket of possibilities that were placed in us before we were ever born. The very presence of those desires is confirmation that you have all that it takes to bring them to life. You may not be able to see it but all the resources, all of the connections and all of the people that you need to execute this plan will show up, in their proper order and at the proper time for exactly the right reason. You just have to trust the process while you continue to work the plan. You have to keep working long enough, doing the right things in the right sequence and you will arrive. It's not that it will *"show up"* per se because it's always been there. You will simply arrive further down the road on the correct path at your chosen destination. That's where your desire comes from. The pulling, if you will, towards that thing that already exists and is just sitting there idly waiting for you to arrive.

These ideals created the pattern of thought that we build our lives on today.

STORY TIME:

Imagine that going through life is like being a passenger on a runaway horse and carriage.

The driver is not being responsible with the reins. The carriage and its contents bounce around in every direction. Now, you know very well how to steer the carriage. You have much experience and skill in its maneuvers, but you lack the confidence to grab control of the unruly situation. Soak that in … you're right there with all that's needed but no gumption to grab what's yours and take control. It's your life at stake and on your call, it's left in the hands of someone who doesn't care.

Grab. The. Damn. Reins!!!!! Sheesh!!!

You are always in the driver's seat in your life. Always. There will never be a time, no matter the circumstances, that you will be out of control. All that happens around you and within you stems from you. Stay in that mindset.

If you are in a situation where you are waiting for someone else's move or response, take the initiative and respond, or contact someone new to handle that for you. Never ever let someone else's emotions or the possibility of someone else's anger keep you from staying on track and driving your own life. You can be polite and firm at the same time. Focus and stay true to your ultimate goal. If it means ruffling someone else's feather, accept that and do it anyway. I promise you will thank yourself later.

Hurt feelings should never keep you from doing what is right. A person's response to you voting for yourself will tell you all you need to know about further communication with them. Never hold back your authenticity because you also hold back finding out who's really in your corner.

Stop saying you don't believe you can; just try. Even if it all blows up, at least you went down fighting. The elements point to you meeting a tragic end if you don't step in so at least, give it a go.

In our youth, we make silent pacts with ourselves that we carry into adulthood and even pass on to others as ideals.

matrix, *noun*

:something within or from which something else originates, develops, or takes form

THE MATRIX OF THOUGHT

Your matrix is where your new thought patterns or thought life develop. The tricks and tools I give you will be your matrix. It is where the good thoughts you want most will originate and develop. Be open to it, not blocking out any possibility, and let it work for you.

The Breakdown:

> Your thoughts come from your past:

- experiences

- encounters

- exposure

- caregivers

Basically, every time you experienced an emotion for the first time you received a message that stuck with you. That message resurfaces when you are put in situations that trigger it. Sometimes that resurfacing serves you well and sometimes it does not. You get to decide. By grabbing it when it resurfaces, you command it to go in the direction that suits you. That is true for both good and bad, positive and negative.

"Why would I want something to suit me in a negative way Alana?"

is what I'm sure you're asking. We often find comfort in sameness and familiarity. No matter how destructive the pattern, the repetitiveness seems comfortable to us. We've done it so long we don't even have to think about it. It's why women stay in abusive relationships and why countless other stay in careers they hate. Essentially, we habitually believe that where we are, no matter how destructive, is better than the unknown somewhere else. We are afraid that starting over is so much more painful than working with the scraps we have. The clear truth is that you are not starting over at all. You are setting out on a new path with all the experience you've gained and lessons you've learned. It's like moving to another company for a job. You may be starting over at a new position or even in an entirely new field, but you bring with you all of the career experience that you've gathered over the years.

REFLECTIVE EXERCISE

List 5 traditions you observed as a kid growing up

List 2 to 3 of your primary caregivers from your childhood.

Now, list 5 positive characteristics of each.

Now, list 5 negative characteristics of each.

Study the positive and negative similarities of past caregivers and present relationships. This goes for personal and professional.

Through this, you can see how you both attract and choose friendships, courtships and relationships unknowingly based on your experiences from childhood. This works also in other areas of choice. All of it comes from a place that existed before today. Subsequently, it all can be altered based on new choices from today.

CHAPTER 3
THE AFTERMATH OF THOSE THOUGHTS

Aftermath;

(noun)

1. something that results or follows from an event, especially one of a disastrous or unfortunate nature; consequence

2. the consequences or aftereffects of a significant unpleasant event.

3. a new growth of grass following one or more mowings, which may be grazed, mowed, or plowed under.

Staying in this vein of thought can be destructive to the big and small things in our lives. We find ourselves in places we hate, with people we don't like, doing things we don't love. The mystery solved is that we actually got ourselves there with our thoughts. The beauty of that is, if you got yourself there, then you can get yourself out.

Our thoughts are not as illusive and basic as we think they are.

There is a very clear picture that is created based on what we chose to think on. I hear you, I hear you. You're saying,

"Alana, my thoughts just pop into my head. I don't control them. They're just there!"

Well, that couldn't be further from the truth. Once a thought comes into your consciousness, you are in control of where it goes from there. You get to decide the ending.

Let's take the thought of being single for example. When the thought enters your mind about how hard it is to be single, it is you that allows it to roll into a **superior consciousness** that you'll never find the right person.

superior consciousness, *noun*

:the highest state of awareness

:relating to mentality, it is your most in-tuned deliberate thoughts with the ability to see and understand all that is around you

Each thought after that just lines up directly with whatever you pick out and play in your mind as true. The thought that you're getting too old to get married or you're not as willing to partner up as you used to be is just the fruit of that first negative thought you accepted as true. You have to be more intentional about those thoughts. As soon as you think it, your next move is to think about being single the way you actually prefer it to be. Picture all the great parts of your life as they currently exist. Next, you can take that contentment and begin to build the married life you would like to have. Think of it as if there were no limits. The point is to stop, even if only for a few seconds, divert your mind to what it is you actually want your life to look like. If you're saying,

"But I don't want to be single," or *"I want to visualize being married,"*

then consider this. You must first become fully comfortable with where you already are, optimize the possibilities where you are currently planted to get all the good stuff that you need to take with you into matrimony.

Even though I used the example of being single and wanting to be married, this idea works in any area you are trying to achieve. Job stress? Then visualize yourself being able to handle and flourish despite the stress level. Focus on all the creative steps you can take to make your days more enjoyable. Visualize a huge 300-ton anvil falling on top of that super annoying coworker or boss every time you see them. Get you a really super-duper, cool coffee mug or tea cup to look forward to. Put an inspiring picture in a frame and put it on your desk. All these things will change your thoughts, make the stress more manageable and create a space for you to begin mentally downloading all the possibilities of a new job opportunity if that is what you chose. BE INTENTIONAL!

Your thoughts are kind of like a mischievous little puppy. If left unattended and not properly trained, they will wreak havoc in areas you never even considered were up for grabs on the kaos wheel. You can even find yourself in life threatening situations because of your lack of control in that area.

The detrimental thing about thoughts is that once you meditate on them long enough, they are no longer thoughts. They actually become reality…Your reality. The rest of the world can know a completely different version, but you have built your thoughts around this pseudo truth and are now making moves based on it.

REALITY CHECK:

If you have reason to believe your boyfriend is cheating on you due to lies you've caught him in, not being where he said he would be, being with people he said he wouldn't be, then no amount of visualization is going to make him faithful. Get on your Big Girl bike, the one without the training wheels, and go do what you already know you need to do. Visualization is made to control your own actions not the actions of others. This ain't voodoo, Boo Boo!

Back to business …

Not having control of your thoughts and allowing them to turn into improper actions can actually cost you your life.

STORY TIME:

Elaine tells us her account of what tragedy can happen when you don't follow your instincts. "On a regular day in Autumn,

I arrived alone at my place of work to open the donut shop. It was pretty early so my brain was still trying to wake up. I was in a brain fog. I did notice a few things that seemed odd. One was that the shop owner from across the alley seemed to be driving a different car to work and was earlier than normal. Also he was backed in. I also noticed that the trash can that is usually in front of the back door had been moved. I did feel it was weird, but I didn't overanalyze it. I unlocked the door and after I opened it, I immediately realized the alarm wasn't going off and it shocked me. It was like all of the out-of-place things I noticed came together and slapped me awake. I started to back up from the door and I bolted to my car. I think I started driving away before I was fully in the car. As I sped away, I could see a figure dressed in black pants and a black hoodie running from the building. The police found out that it was one of my new coworkers. He was planning on kidnapping me and taking me to a hotel room to rape me. I made a promise to myself to never overlook my instinct again."

Elaine was not doing a great job of trusting herself. When you practice mindful thinking you get focused. Your focus is on the solutions that come to you based on being so connected to your thoughts. You notice things like Elain did and act on them.

In this case missing out on these clues could have very well cost her natural life. We do the very same thing on a regular basis in most cases. We may not always put our natural life in danger. We do endanger our professional life our personal life and even our spiritual life by second-guessing what is right *in front of us. We do this because we are focused on things that are not serving us.*

Take a lesson from Elaine and trust yourself more. Acknowledge what you see right in front of you and give yourself the permission to accept it as true even if it means making you look silly. The truth is the majority of the time your first thought is your correct one. Learn to go with it and trust yourself more.

We often believe untrue things about ourselves that direct our choices. When the thoughts that support those untruths come into our mind we constantly go over them and make decisions that support those untruths. We choose jobs that don't fulfill us, we choose relationships that don't nurture us and we cut off our own joy because of it.

Women will make a decision as life altering as who their spouse/ significant other will be based on the idea that there is a shortage of good men or women out there or the idea that her age has something to do with their eligibility of love and support from a soulmate.

If you don't understand that you are worth enough to have exactly what you want and you don't have to settle for less, then you believe a lie. There is no mistake you've made, nothing you lack that can keep you from having and deserving exactly what you desire.

Oh, and a bit of advice: stop worrying about being so damn nice!!! (There ... I said it! Whew!)

REFLECTIVE EXERCISE

1. What are some consequences you've had to live with in your life that you felt were out of your control?

2. When you think back to the time leading up to those events, was there anything you could've done differently so as to not arrive in that place?

3. Was the outcome exactly what you were afraid of all along?

If you had focused on something other than what you feared would happen it could have revealed more choices. Those extra choices very possibly could have put you on a different path.

CHAPTER 4
THE REMEDY

Remedy:

(noun)

1. a medicine, application, or treatment that relieves or cures a disease

2. something that corrects or counteracts

(verb)

1. provide or serve as a remedy for

Take a minute and sit back. No, really, sit back in your seat for about 60 seconds with your eyes closed. BUT NOT IF YOU'RE DRIVING (you should probably put this down if you are). Now, just free think for that time. Don't force yourself to focus on one particular thought. Just allow them to flow in and out of your mental viewfinder. If you come across a thought that you don't like, just pass it through to the other side of your view and make room for the next thought to come in. The opposite goes for a good thought. When one comes through, hold it for a few moments. Look at it. Feel it wash over you. Breathe it in and stay with it's good feeling for a few extra moments. Then allow it to pass on to make room for more. Repeat this over and over for one minute or for as long as you can.

After some time, it will become fun for you. It's a lot like dreaming of what you would do if you won the lottery. You have to do it without limits. Do it as if money didn't matter, geographical location was not a factor and background or experience wasn't involved.

It really is a very simple process. That's why it's so easy to not do it. The easiest stuff can be the hardest to be consistent with. You can also practice this in mini-sessions, moment by moment. If you're driving along and seem to only be focused on the tough meeting ahead, divert your mind to what happens after the meeting, when it's all over and your presentation was a success. Maybe there are high-fives being thrown, promotions being mentioned or it's simply you, quietly sitting in your office, staring out the window with a smile of confidence, knowing you did your best and gave them exactly what they asked for. The main thing is to spend deliberate time on the thoughts of those things that you actually want to show up in your life.

When you think of a job, only focus on all the things you do want, not the things you hate about your current job. You see, we call forth things from the shadows based on how we govern our thoughts. Both the good things we want and the bad things we don't want are sitting there like soldiers waiting to be called to attention with their marching orders. We decide with our thoughts who's up next for deployment.

STORY TIME:

Connie was on her way home from a long day of work. She was so tired, yet she dreaded going home.

She and her husband were fighting into the wee hours of the morning. While she was sore from his physical abuse, her mind was in pain from the emotional abuse.

She couldn't make sense of her life any longer. Why did she stay? Why did she make excuses for his behavior? How could she rationalize allowing someone to treat her this way when she'd never allow it to happen to her daughter? Connie's mind was in a state of total confusion. Who am I, she wondered. How can I get back to the girl who knew what she wanted and wasn't afraid to get it?

Connie had become so accustomed to defending him, to others and herself:

"He only does it when he drinks."
"It's really only when he's stressed from work."
"We do have a lot of good times."

These were the things she told herself in order to justify her decision to stay.

In 20 years with Ray, Connie has endured countless broken bones, numerous bruises, scratches and sprains. Most of her family and friends don't come around anymore because their presence seems to prompt something in Ray that usually ends in a bad time for Connie.

Even though Connie was never exposed to domestic violence growing up, she never had a real relationship with her father. Something about the lack of that relationship told her she wasn't good enough. It taught her that she should settle and take what she could get in relation to a man.

Connie truly believed that at the age of 36 she was too old to attract a good man. She had convinced herself long ago that there was a shortage of good men and not only did a good men not want a woman past 30 but he certainly didn't want a woman with children. Every time she got to thinking about having the courage to leave Ray and choose her own sanity, she switched to her reality that there was no one out there who would want her.

All Connie could think of is how hard it would be starting over without Ray. After all, they've been together more than half her life. Leaving would change everything and completely disrupt her daily routines. Right now, her routines actually bring her comfort. They seem to be the one thing that she has control over. They give her a sense of stability even though everything around her is completely out of order. She has gotten to the point we're staying where she is in the middle of danger feels more comfortable than moving into the unknown.

Halfway home, Connie's palms begin to sweat. On a recent morning news show, a woman talked at length about how changing her thoughts changed her life. Caught in a desperate situation, she began to think in great detail about the good things that would happen if she made the move to start again.

She visualized in so much detail that she could smell the scent of the fancy perfume she would wear when she got a new job in a new town with a new company in the field she'd always wanted. Imagining doing the same thing sent butterflies flying in Connie's stomach.

But she was desperate and in the car halfway from home she started to think differently. She remembered some of the dreams she had for her career and for her children. Dreams that Ray had often made fun of. Dreams she had long since let go because it seemed easier than going against her aggressor. Connie pictured herself driving into the parking lot of the company where her dream job existed. And she smiled.

Arriving at home, she found an angry Ray. He'd had trouble at work and he was in the mood to take it out on everyone else.

Connie did what she could not to set Ray off. She remained within the behavioral guidelines that he deemed acceptable. She even had sex with him that night, all the while holding on to the vivid picture of a different life. With it came the stirrings of a new resolve.

Morning came and found Ray still in a cross state, but more importantly a nonviolent one. Connie got up early to get things together for the kids to head to school. She wanted to make sure they were quiet in their rooms while Ray got ready for work. Before she knew it he was out the door. So many things ran through her mind. What about my job? What about the bazaar committee meeting at church? Suddenly, none of those things seemed more important than her safety and the well-being of her children.

Connie took a few items of her own and a few items for her children and packed them into the trunk of her car. She was scared to death. But that visualization of freedom pushed her to keep moving forward. As the kids finished their breakfast and then loaded their backpacks into the backseat Connie decided she would try to make this fun for them which would lighten a little of her stress and anxiety. She told the kids that they all had been working so hard and needed a break. She told them they were going on a secret adventure. Her eight-year-old daughter immediately replied, **"I hope dad's not coming."** *Connie's chest sunk. It was just what she needed to tie her to the reality that this was a trip that was long overdue. She wasn't certain where she was going but she was absolutely sure where she wasn't staying.*

In the weeks that followed, she found refuge a couple states away at her sister's house. Many of the people she thought were friends deserted her. But she held onto the vision of what her life could be. Many nights she cried herself to sleep. The road ahead seemed long, but she was always comforted knowing she was out of Ray's presence and closer to the life she really wanted.

Days turned into weeks, months, and then years and Connie found herself and her children stronger wiser and more confident each day. Helping her move on was going public with her story. Exposing Ray was something she always knew she had to do because it was one of the key details she remembered from the interview with the woman she had seen many months ago. The woman spoke about how exposing an abuser can embarrass them to the point of hiding out or just retreating from their mission to try to control you.

Connie did get her life in order. She realized that she wasn't starting over but rather graduating to a new level and taking all the experience, knowledge and skills with her that she had gathered through the years. She hasn't officially gotten her dream job but is surely closer than she has ever been. She is at least working in the field and acquiring extra certifications that will make the transition more profitable.

Connie almost paid for her desperate way of thinking with her life. That's the direction she was headed in. Nothing around her changed until she changed the handling of her thoughts. Also, one good thought lead to another and then another and then a new life landscape. It put her in a place where she could quiet the noise of others' opinions about her divorce and focus on what was truer than any idealistic view on marriage; that she was living a dreadful, loveless existence and nothing was OK about that. Changing her thought process made her realize that no matter what was on the other side of this change it wasn't worse than the fate of staying.

Don't let others' ideals trap you in despair. Also understand that physical abuse and name calling or degradation are not the only reasons to leave a marriage. Any feelings of being unloved or devalued warrants a conversation, setting of boundaries, setting of expectations and a plan of action to make permanent changes. If the lack of love, respect and value grows and or persists, an exit strategy should be considered.

REFLECTION EXERCISE

1. Have you ever been in a situation where you felt helpless?

_____

_____

_____

_____

2. Did you find that once you started the process of getting through it that it wasn't as tough as you anticipated?

_____

_____

_____

_____

3. Think of a current challenge.

    1. How can you change the way you think about it?

    2. What are some things you can do differently to progress in a positive direction?

    3. Are you willing to ask for help to get past this challenge?

CHAPTER 5

THE PRESCRIPTION
Your Matrix of Thought

Prescription:

(noun)

1. the action of laying down authoritative rules or directions

2. a written direction for a therapeutic or corrective agent specifically : one for the preparation and use of a medicine

(verb)

1. something (such as a recommendation) resembling a doctor's prescription

1. Make A Plan

2. Cultivate Your Dream Space

3. Be Intentional

4. Be Diligent

5. Take Off The Training Wheels (Dream without limits)

Make A Plan just as if you were trying to tackle any other task. Plan your thoughts for the year based on what you want and when. Put them in a cool notebook or a fancy calendar.

Cultivate Your Dream Space by "laying out" your thoughts before bed. Take a look at your thought layout before bed. Even if you just glance at it, that's still helpful.

Be Intentional. Turn on your Can-Do Mindset. You will deliberately and intentionally start your day with the right kind of thoughts. You don't even have to get out of bed for this. When you begin this routine, you will refer to what you have mapped out. Having it by your bedside will be essential. It will also help if you are in a hurry during your morning routine.

Be Diligent. You can prop it up on your mirror as you brush your teeth, put on makeup or coif your hair. There is nothing to memorize. You're simply training your brain to manifest thoughts that will create the life you want by looking over images or words that represent what you want.

Take Off The Training Wheels & Dream Without Limits. You are not limited by resources, time, age, familial status, geographic location, or economic orientation. If the crazy thought pops into your head that you'll be the CEO of a multimillion-dollar company that YOU created, just go with that. Build on that crazy thought. Thoughts are free. No one can place boundaries on our thoughts. We can just sit back and think, think, think.

REALITY CHECK:

This will not prevent bad or challenging things in your life, but it will give you the tools you need to successfully navigate those occurrences.

Now listen, you will find yourself at times saying, ***"Screw that thinking shit! I'm pissed!"*** and that is perfectly fine. You are allowed to feel genuine emotion as a reaction to something. You are even allowed to have a FIVE-MINUTE PITY PARTY. You're just not allowed to stay there. Give yourself space and permission to feel the emotion, whether it's heartbreak, disappointment or even sheer and utter pride (we sometimes need permission to be happy for ourselves; that humble bull is played out). After your pitiful time is up, you need to move. Focus on what you want, not what is around you. I'm sure you're saying,

"Alana, you just don't understand how he hurt me," or ***"But I almost died,"*** or ***"It could have ended my career,"***

or even, "My life will never be the same after this." To that, I say, "Perfect!" that means you are primed and ready for a shift. It means your life was in such a place that you need to almost lose it to gain the awareness needed to make a change.

Your tragedy is nothing new. There are thousands who can tell a story 10 times worse than yours, and they made it out. It's all up to you. It's up to you to put your phone down, log off of social media for a moment and get up from the comfy couch. Your next level doesn't care that you had a rough day at work. Your rough work days want you to sulk in your corner of the bed from mental exhaustion. The more you continue doing what you're doing, you will keep creating the exact same life you already have. You know, the one you need a vacation from and can't seem to get enough peace in.

As I sit here and type this book for you, I do it with victory over all hurt, pain, disappointment and depression. I allowed myself to sit in that, year after year, before I got up out of my hole and turned on the light. The very idea and urge to write this book came from me mentally breaking free and wanting to live on my next level. I want to take everyone with me to the better side that I fought so hard to arrive on. The view is so much better here. The air is cleaner, and my head is clearer. I've done a lot of work and I still have plenty to do.

However, I now get to do it with joy, hope, and the peace and confidence that it's all going to work out. I'm mentally prepared for the tough times ahead. I am mature in my thinking. I forecast for challenges because not only do I know they will come, I welcome them. I welcome them because I know firsthand that the hard stuff is what grows you.

The hard stuff is what fortifies your resolve to do whatever it is you do. The hard stuff comes to remind me that I am built to withstand and built to be greater. Afterall, my posterity depend on me to be the greatest that I can, so they have a higher rung to start form. How I handle what's ahead, good, bad, or neutral, is a test I intend to pass. I also intend to give myself the grace to fall and the courage to get back up.

STORY TIME:

There's a woman living in a small suburb of a larger Metropolitan city. We'll call her Teresa.

Teresa's life appears to be all in order, at least it looks that way from the outside. She's usually the life of the party, she's always been a snappy dresser, she and her husband adore each other and their children are healthy and happy.

Seemingly Teresa doesn't really have any major obstacles in her life. Sure she's put on some weight since her younger days, but that's not uncommon. She wears a lot of hats and seems to be good at all of her roles. But there is one problem. She feels overwhelmed.

She often beats herself up for not being able to make the cupcakes from scratch that her son needs for his 100-day school party. She frequently looks down on herself for not being able to keep a perfectly clean home. She doesn't realize that she puts the importance of her family and her outside activities before her own self-care. Instead, she labels herself as lazy for not being able to keep up. Looking out at the lives of others, her view is that everyone seems to have it all together except her. None of the positive things that her husband and loved ones say about her seem to penetrate her idea of personal worthlessness.

Teresa is in a rut and unknowingly depressed. She is sinking fast. She often considers scaling back on her extra responsibilities but quickly jumps back in line with the idea that she's just being immature and that letting go of anything will decrease her value in the eyes of those who love her. She presses on and tries to hold it all together. Teresa is grossly unfulfilled. She has found herself in an environment where there are a lot of people who are takers. Many of the individuals around her, including those whom she respects and looks up to, often call on her to go above and beyond the call of duty. Considering many of those things to be an honor, Teresa almost always obliges. She hasn't yet figured out that all these worthwhile causes are stripping her of her sanity and her independent thinking.

One crisp clear morning, Teresa begins to once again consider dropping some responsibilities. This time she gets the revelation that doing so in a few areas would free her to focus more on the education and advancement of her children. When she shares the idea with her husband, he is completely on board. Even though this decision will decrease a small bit of their household income, she eventually decides to go forward with it. That tiny taste of freedom sparks more free thinking on her part.

Teresa brainstorms all the worthwhile things she will be able to do with her children and her husband once she clears more tasks from her schedule. There's a change being created in her thinking. Instead of thinking constantly of the negative things that she perceived would come out of decreasing her commitments, she thought of the upside. Teresa began to fall in love with the idea of being less committed to outside responsibilities that mostly took from her time with her family.

It wasn't easy. You see, Teresa had formed a habit of clearing off her plate of commitments and then adding smaller, less intrusive ones. To her, this was okay at first. But after a while that familiar feeling of overwhelm begin to set back in. This time, it seemed a little more bitter than the last. Teresa thought she had figured it out and was on her way to total freedom. What she didn't realize was that clearing off one major responsibility then adding on three smaller ones was actually worse than where she started. She also developed a habit of allowing the reactions of others to dictate what responsibility she accepted or rejected.

Even as an outspoken forthright woman, Teresa still found herself in positions where she couldn't say no for fear of the backlash. She all too often agreed to responsibilities because the discomfort of adding more to her plate seemed easier than handling the disapproval of the person she would have to say no to. She recognized she was in a vicious cycle. She knew she needed to do something about it.

The next few months were very tough for Teresa. She carried a lot of guilt, feeling like she was disappointing the people around her by voting for herself. Sure, she maintained the revelation and moved forward but it took some time for her to realize her true worth and the honor that it actually was for others to be part of her life.

Teresa began to focus more heavily on all that could happen positively by making these changes in her life. The more she did that the more it seemed like creative answers and important outlets began to show up in her life. She would eventually have a conversation, random of course, with a friend that brought up how seeing a therapist changed a lot of things in her life. Teresa wasn't too sure about therapy. I mean after all, shouldn't you just be able to go to church and get all the advice you need? Shouldn't you just be able to pray it away? If nothing else this conversation made Teresa at least consider therapy as an option. In the days that followed, it seemed like everywhere she looked there was more and more information about therapy and talking to someone professionally about your problems. There were random social media posts from friends and random articles and podcasts that just popped up on her timelines.

The whole thing opened up a conversation to the degree that she even researched her insurance benefits for mental health. She was shocked at how easily accessible seeing a therapist was. Her insurance covered almost 80% of the therapist fees. She immediately called and got a personalized list of therapists in her area. She picked through the list then called all the numbers until she narrowed down the one she felt was right for her. If proved to be a perfect fit.

Teresa would begin regular visits once, sometimes twice, a week in the beginning. She felt like she had her entire community behind her because there was starting to be quite a buzz about mental health, emotional wellness and self-care. The guilt that she once felt in taking better care of herself turned into a feeling of empowerment. She was now taking her own advice. She had countless times encouraged other women to be nicer to themselves, to give themselves more grace and to trust themselves more. It took a little time, a lot of understanding and the right amount of self-love for her to see a change in the environment around her.

Without warning, her relationships shifted. Some people fell off completely, others' positions changed and still others leaned in closer to sprinkle an extra amount of love and support for this new journey she was on.

Teresa was shocked. She had too many times believed that no one could support her, undergird her, or love her the way she did to others. Thankfully she was so wrong. Among the changes was rekindling old friendships and redefining current ones. Life was starting to become fun again. There were possibilities in life that became new again. There were dreams that she had pushed off and some she even gave up on that now had a new lease on life. She even considered writing a book (wink, wink).

Teresa's life turned around. Within a year she was experiencing a life that she wanted and not one that she settled for. Finally detaching herself from the opinions of others, she began to soar. Everyone around her felt the vibes of the woman she was becoming. She began to move differently, think differently, and talk differently.

Teresa didn't depend on others to change her. She took the authority and changed the only thing she could: herself. She didn't do that by waiting around for the right time or wasting resources that weren't advancing her. The number one thing that set the wheel in motion was how she changed the thoughts that filled her mind. It didn't cost her any money. She didn't have to reach outside herself. She didn't even have to go out of her way. All she did was toss the thoughts of what she didn't want and reached down to pull up the thoughts that painted the picture of what she did want.

Teresa realized that her value and the value of her life was based on being and not doing. She learned that there was no way of earning her status but that if she never corrected another mistake and if she never made another advancement she would still, right now, where she already was, be worthy of all the love that she gives out and then some.

She was finally able to live in the understanding that every step she took no matter in what direction she was of high value and anyone would be fortunate to be a part of her life. That knowledge freed her in ways she never imagined.

Today Teresa is an author. She's tapped into the resources and avenues on how to do what she's done her whole life, and that's bring hope, encouragement and a plan of action to all types of women all around the world.

By now, you've probably figured out that Teresa's real name is Alana Higginbotham. Yup, that's me and there is so much more yet to be told. But we have plenty of time for that. Because you and me, we're going to be doing this for a long long time.

I plan to help you, your friends, and everyone you know live the life they want by sharing my life and showing you the possibilities in the process.

I've got some pretty big goals that extend far past this subject matter, and I plan to achieve them all. I already know it's going to be hard, and I welcome that. Because I know I have the tools to get through and the chutzpah to never give up.

Stay with me and we can work this thing together while building a legacy that will last forever.

Let me help you leave your mark.

I don't know if I can convey on these pages how much I want this for you. I've laid awake at night and cried for something bigger than me to help me change my life. It only worked when I got help. I only got help when I changed my mental dialogue. But it's your turn now...

GO BE GREAT!

FINAL CHECK:

It's not going to always be easy. Some things will take a lot more focus and fortitude than others. It's okay, that's expected. This is simply because there are some thought processes that are more deeply rooted than others. Further, there are some so deeply rooted that you haven't even identified them as issues and still some that you don't even know exist. It's all going to be all right in time, if you work at it.

Give yourself the proper amount of space you need. Don't set unrealistic goals. Get yourself a therapist AND an accountability partner. You didn't get to this place all by yourself so it's going to take some teamwork to get out of it.

Be patient with yourself. Stay focused on healing your thoughts. Even a small victory is still a few steps forward and a few new mindsets closer to your next level.

You've got this. The fact that you're reading this says you know there's a problem and you want to do something about it.

Trust the process. Trust yourself. Push forward. Push beyond that which is beyond you. Your new mindset has already started taking root.

Welcome To Better!

REFLECTIVE EXERCISE

1. Have you ever received advice and thought to yourself, "Yeah but my situation is different?"

2. Is there anything in your life that you've resolved to just accept because you feel like you can't change it?

3. Do you currently feel like you value yourself at the level that you should?

4. Repeat this to yourself three times out loud:

   I am already who I need to be to acquire and maintain the life that I want. The provisions that are necessary to experience the life that I want are not something that I need to achieve or acquire.

Everything I need knowingly and unknowingly is simply further down the path. As long as I proceed forward I will arrive at precisely the right place in precisely the right moment with precisely the right tools. I am already where I want to be!

Quotes That Can Help

"Never take advice from someone you wouldn't trade places with"

~ unknown

"Never give up what you believe"

~Daymond John

"I think it's only failure if you put the word failure on it. I think it's part of the process of learning."

~Daymond John

"You are not born a winner, you are not born a loser. You are born a chooser."

~Daymond John

"Either you run the day, or the day runs you."

~Jim Rohn

"Discipline is the bridge between goals and accomplishments."

~Jim Rohn

"Happiness is not something you postpone for the future; it is something you design for the present."

~Jim Rohn

"If you don't like how things are, change it! You're not a tree."

~Jim Rohn

"Be thankful for what you have; you'll end up having more. If you concentrate on what you don't have, you will never, ever have enough."

~Oprah Winfrey

"The biggest adventure you can ever take is to live the life of your dreams."

~ Oprah Winfrey

"Think like a queen. A queen is not afraid to fail. Failure is another stepping stone to greatness."

~ Oprah Winfrey

"The more you praise and celebrate your life, the more there is in life to celebrate."

~ Oprah Winfrey

"Passion is energy. Feel the power that comes from focusing on what excites you."

~ Oprah Winfrey

"Lots of people want to ride with you in the limo, but what you want is someone who will take the bus with you when the limo breaks down."

~ Oprah Winfrey

TIPS FOR YOUR JOURNEY:

- Be prepared for challenges

    - Remember this is not just the snap of a finger. Its forming new habits. You WILL slip back into old habits. Just redirect and get back on track.

- No matter what, no one can do you better than you.

    - Flaws and all, you are perfectly equipped to do whatever you desire to.

- When you are faced with a challenge, ask yourself this question: Is it within my power to change this situation?

    - You'll find that most of the time the answer is no. The only way you can change something is if your personal actions started it in the first place. You can only do what is in your power to do. You can only do what changes you.

- You are not alone in this.

    - Many people with far less than you and far more excuses have overcome even tougher obstacles.

    - You're not the first person to go through this.

- Turn your pity into preparation
    - Yes this will be tough but not always.
    - Celebrate even the smallest of victories.
    - If a challenge arises or regression occurs, pause to take a deep breath and go back to the plan.

- You have always been more than enough to complete the journey. You simply figured it out a little later.

- A crucial part of the journey is pausing to clap for yourself, cultivate relationships, care for your physical and mental well-being, and curating downtime.

ABOUT AUTHOR

Alana takes her own personal experiences and delivers a message that anyone can use to help their growth. As a Mental Wellness Coach she helps you turn your anxiety into opportunity. She shares a bit of her own life's challenges and the strategies she used to overcome them.

As an author, public speaker and corporate trainer Alana Higginbotham can infuse her powerful, positive energy into your daily methods to enrich and elevate your life's experience.

To stay in touch with Alana and/or book her for your next event use the info below.

Website: www.alanahigginbotham.com

Email: info@alanahigginbotham.com

Instagram: @AlanaHigginbotham

Facebook: Alana Higginbotham

Twitter: @arhigginbotham

LinkedIn: Alana Higginbotham

Made in the USA
Middletown, DE
24 February 2019